AS in a Week

Business Studies

D0178195

Steve Dalton,
Abbey College, Manchester
Series Editor: Kevin Byrne

SUCCESS OR YOUR MONEY BACK

Letts' market leading series AS in a Week gives you everything you need for exam success. We're so confident that they're the best revision books you can buy that if you don't make the grade we will give you your money back!

HERE'S HOW IT WORKS

Register the Letts AS in a Week guide you buy by writing to us within 28 days of purchase with the following information:
- Name
- Address
- Postcode
- Subject of AS in a Week book bought

Please include your till receipt

To make a **claim**, compare your results to the grades below. If any of your grades qualify for a refund, make a claim by writing to us within 28 days of getting your results, enclosing a copy of your original exam slip. If you do not register, you won't be able to make a claim after you receive your results.

CLAIM IF...

You are an AS (Advanced Subsidiary) student and do not get grade E or above.

You are a Scottish Higher level student and do not get a grade C or above.

This offer is not open to Scottish students taking SCE Higher Grade, or Intermediate qualifications.

Letts Educational
Aldine Place
London W12 8AW
Tel: 020 8740 2266
Fax: 020 8743 8451
e-mail: mail@lettsed.co.uk
website: www.letts-education.com

Registration and claim address:
Letts Success or Your Money Back Offer, Letts Educational, Aldine Place, London W12 8AW

TERMS AND CONDITIONS

1. Applies to the Letts AS in a Week series only
2. Registration of purchases must be received by Letts Educational within 28 days of the purchase date
3. Registration must be accompanied by a valid till receipt
4. All money back claims must be received by Letts Educational within 28 days of receiving exam results
5. All claims must be accompanied by a letter stating the claim and a copy of the relevant exam results slip
6. Claims will be invalid if they do not match with the original registered subjects
7. Letts Educational reserves the right to seek confirmation of the level of entry of the claimant
8. Responsibility cannot be accepted for lost, delayed or damaged applications, or applications received outside of the stated registration/claim timescales
9. Proof of posting will not be accepted as proof of delivery
10. Offer only available to AS students studying within the UK
11. SUCCESS OR YOUR MONEY BACK is promoted by Letts Educational, Aldine Place, London W12 8AW
12. Registration indicates a complete acceptance of these rules
13. Illegible entries will be disqualified
14. In all matters, the decision of Letts Educational will be final and no correspondence will be entered into

First published 2000

British Library Cataloguing in Publication Data
A CIP record for this book is available from the British Library.

ISBN 1 84085 367 0

Prepared by *specialist* publishing services, Milton Keynes

Printed in Italy

Letts Educational Limited is a division of Granada Learning Limited, part of the Granada Media Group

Stakeholders and Objectives

Test your knowledge

1 Objectives are _____ or _____ that define the purpose or reasons for the business to exist.

2 Objectives form a key ingredient of any business _____, which represents a plan for the future.

3 Objectives are important because they can provide a sense of _____ or common purpose for a business, enabling all participants in that business to unify around them.

4 A useful distinction can be made between _____ objectives, which define the aims of the whole business, and lower-level operational objectives such as departmental sales targets.

5 _____ _____ is the most widely quoted and understood of the various possible business objectives, but there are also several others that may be important.

6 A stakeholder is defined as a person or organisation that has an _____ in the activities or outcomes of a business.

7 Commentators sympathetic to the 'stakeholder philosophy' believe that businesses which embrace the demands of all their stakeholder groups are more likely to behave _____ .

8 Behavioural theory sees business practice as being a consequence of _____ between the various stakeholder groups. Some of them will be more powerful than others.

Answers

1 goals, targets 2 strategy 3 direction 4 corporate 5 Profit maximisation 6 interest 7 responsibly 8 conflict

✔ **If you got them all right, skip to page 6**

Improve your knowledge

 1 Objectives are goals or targets that represent the aims or aspirations of the business. When there are several objectives, they are not always wholly compatible with each other. Conflicts between objectives can occur.

 2 Objectives are an integral part of any business strategy. Strategies are long term plans which are intended to guide the business in future years and provide the means by which the objectives are to be realised.

 3 A greater sense of direction should be present in a business if there is an explicit awareness of the objectives. Targets are there to motivate managers and employees to achieve the overall corporate objectives.

4 Corporate objectives define the aims of the whole business or company. These should be distinguished from the subordinate and lower level targets of individual departments. However, there should be an overall harmony and compatibility between the various levels of objectives. Operational objectives should work together to fulfil the corporate objectives.

 5 Profit maximisation is usually the first aim to be found on any list of business objectives. This is the constant quest to widen the gap between revenues and costs. However, there has been much debate amongst economists as to whether firms actually do aim primarily for profit maximisation. Alternative theories have been based on the view that in large companies, profit is important until it is at a satisfactory level. After that, it is argued, other objectives become more important.

 6 A person or group with an interest in the activities or outcomes of a business can be regarded as one of its stakeholders. They are therefore individuals and organisations who may be affected by a business or who may, in turn, influence the business. Some stakeholder groups, for example investors, may have a more direct and obvious relationship with a business than others, such as future generations.

7 It is increasingly argued that businesses that consider the impact of decisions on all their stakeholder groups are more likely to behave responsibly. For example, energy consumption may be limited in order to benefit future generations. Of course, in this example, there is no conflict with the objective of profit maximisation. This will not always be the case.

8 The shareholder or investor stakeholder group is generally regarded as the dominant one in modern UK corporate situations. Sometimes there will be conflict between this and other stakeholders where interests do not coincide, for example in the case of a proposed merger that will lead to job losses. The relative power of different stakeholder groups will change over time. The labour interest, for example, is less influential than it was in the 1970s.

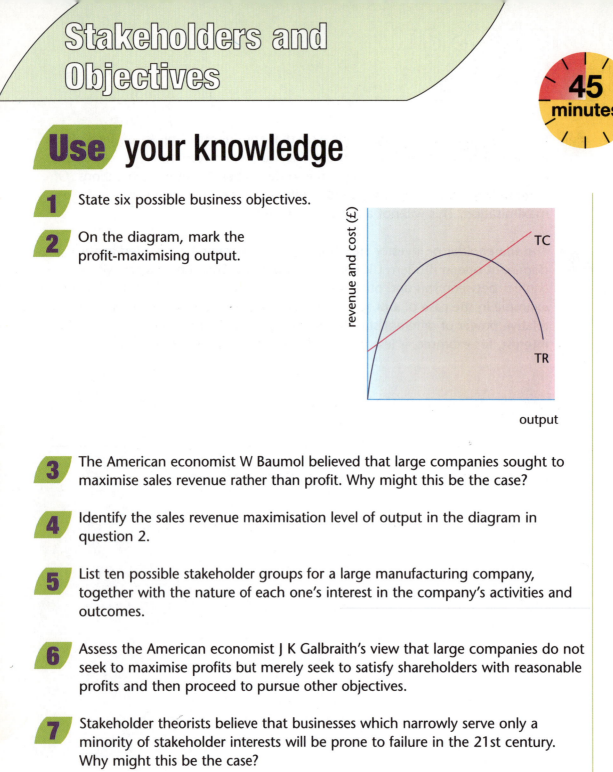

45 minutes

Use your knowledge

Hint

1 State six possible business objectives.

not just profit max

2 On the diagram, mark the profit-maximising output.

3 The American economist W Baumol believed that large companies sought to maximise sales revenue rather than profit. Why might this be the case?

CV

4 Identify the sales revenue maximisation level of output in the diagram in question 2.

5 List ten possible stakeholder groups for a large manufacturing company, together with the nature of each one's interest in the company's activities and outcomes.

cast net wide

6 Assess the American economist J K Galbraith's view that large companies do not seek to maximise profits but merely seek to satisfy shareholders with reasonable profits and then proceed to pursue other objectives.

divorce

7 Stakeholder theorists believe that businesses which narrowly serve only a minority of stakeholder interests will be prone to failure in the 21st century. Why might this be the case?

ethics

Sources of Finance

15 minutes

Test your knowledge

1 Sole traders often have difficulty raising finance because they have little _____ to offer lenders.

2 An important distinction in company finance is between _____ capital and _____ capital.

3 The relative share of fixed-interest (or fixed-dividend) and variable-interest capital within a company's capital structure, is measured by the _____ ratio.

4 Debentures are a popular way for companies to raise long term finance. However, failure to pay the interest due, or to repay the capital sum at the appropriate date, may result in the appointment of a _____.

5 A private limited company's shares are more difficult to dispose of because the restrictions on their transferability make them less _____.

6 A fixed rate of dividend is paid on _____ shares.

7 An invitation to existing shareholders to purchase new shares at a discount price is known as a _____ issue.

8 Raising short term finance by selling sales invoices to a specialist agency is known as debt _____.

Answers

1 security 2 share, loan 3 gearing 4 receiver 5 liquid 6 preference
7 rights 8 factoring

✔ **If you got them all right, skip to page 10**

30 minutes

Improve your knowledge

1 Lenders generally insist on partial or complete security or collateral, in return for any loan finance granted to sole traders. In this way, a legal charge or mortgage is placed on the assets used. Failure to cover the interest or repay the capital at the appropriate time may lead to the repossession of these assets. The problem for sole traders is that they tend to have few assets to offer as security, apart from their main residence.

2 Share capital and loan capital play very different financing roles in companies. Alternative terms are equity or debt capital respectively. Each of these two major categories of long term finance has its own specific characteristics and merits. It is a complex matter of judgement as to which may be preferable in any given situation.

3 The gearing ratio measures the relative proportions of debt and equity capital. There are various possible formulae that can be used to calculate this ratio, but a typical one is:

$$\frac{\text{Loans, debentures and preference shares}}{\text{Total capital}} \times 100\%$$

As debt and equity capital tend to have different expected rates of return, their relative proportions will affect the weighted average cost of capital or discount rate used in investment appraisal computations.

4 A receiver is appointed by creditors with instructions to sell part or all of the company in order to realise funds to repay the creditors. Receivers have legal rights to enter business property and seize assets to sell.

Sources of Finance

 Private limited company shares are not particularly liquid because of the restrictions on their transferability. Other board members may wish to maintain shares within the family and insist on the complete consent of all members before any transfer can be made. Quoted public limited company shares are much more liquid as there is a functioning secondhand market for the shares in the stock market.

 Preference shares contain the right to a fixed rate of dividend. This is often cumulative in that any failure to pay the dividend in one year will have to be made good in subsequent years.

 A rights issue of shares is an inexpensive and popular way for a company to raise new capital. The pre-emption rights to buy are generally at a discount and are granted in proportion to the number of shares an individual already owns in the company.

8 Debt factoring can provide up to 80% of the value of unpaid sales invoices as cash 'up front' for a company. The factoring agency then collects the debt and sends the balance to the client later, after deducting the debt collection and financing fee.

Sources of Finance

Use your knowledge

Hint

1 Describe the information that a bank manager may consider in deciding whether to grant an increase in overdraft facilities to a business customer.

credit-worthy?

2 What are the financial benefits that can accrue to an ordinary shareholder?

income/growth?

3 What are the advantages and disadvantages of debt factoring for a small business?

liquidity or profitability?

4 State four typical characteristics of preference shares.

5 Assess the case for and against the use of debentures as a way of raising new company finance.

risk v cost

6 Describe the risks, from an ordinary shareholder's perspective, of purchasing shares in a highly geared company.

7 Distinguish between revenue expenditure and capital expenditure. Does this have any implications for the method of finance used?

8 State two internal sources of finance.

not shareholders!

15 minutes

Test your knowledge

 1 Breakeven occurs when a firm makes neither a profit nor a loss. It is therefore when contribution exactly covers _____ _____.

 2 Contribution per unit is a key variable. It is defined as _____ _____ minus _____ _____ per unit.

 3 Profit is any surplus of total revenue over total cost. It is thus contribution per unit multiplied by _____ and then _____ _____ are deducted.

 4 When current output exceeds the breakeven output, the firm has a buffer of sales before a loss is made. This buffer is known as the _____ _____ _____.

 5 For special (i.e. one-off) order situations, a firm must calculate whether there is a positive _____ . If there is, the order is potentially profitable.

 6 A simplifying assumption of breakeven is that all units of output produced are sold. It therefore neglects the impact of _____ on the decision-making process.

 7 In breakeven diagrams, both total revenue and total cost schedules tend to be represented as straight lines. This ignores the possibility of _____ _____ _____ being present on both sales and purchases of materials.

Answers

1 fixed costs 2 selling price, variable cost 3 output, fixed costs
4 margin of safety 5 contribution 6 demand
7 economies of scale

✔ **If you got them all right, skip to page 13**

30 minutes

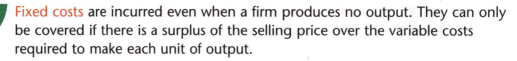

Improve your knowledge

 1 Fixed costs are incurred even when a firm produces no output. They can only be covered if there is a surplus of the selling price over the variable costs required to make each unit of output.

 2 Contribution per unit is an important measure of the difference between a product's selling price and its variable cost.

 3 Profit is what is left after both variable and fixed costs have been deducted from sales revenue. Alternatively it is contribution calculated on output less fixed costs.

 4 The margin of safety measures a firm's exposure to reductions in demand for its product. The smaller the margin, the greater the risk of failing to cover costs.

 5 The firm's normal fixed costs can usually be ignored in special order decisions as these are assumed to be met within normal production. However, any extra fixed costs arising out of the special order will have to be taken into account. The total contribution from the special order must more than cover these for the order to be profitable.

 6 Demand is probably the most important constraint for most firms and therefore it is very unrealistic to assume all output can be sold. Inevitably a firm's stock will tend to fluctuate with movements in the business cycle.

7 Higher levels of sales may require the seller to reduce the selling price. Also, greater purchases of raw material usually lead to a bulk purchasing discount. The effect of such economies of scale would create curves rather than straight lines for cost and revenue.

45 minutes

Use your knowledge

Hint

1   A company, Firezone Ltd, manufactures a single product, 'Cracker'. It has prepared the following budget for its production in the forthcoming year:

	£
Direct material per unit of 'Cracker'	15
Direct labour per unit of 'Cracker'	10
Rent on premises per annum	2 000 000
Business rates per annum	500 000
Depreciation of machinery per annum	1 500 000
Insurance of premises per annum	375 000
Selling price per unit of 'Cracker'	60

Current output is 150 000 'Crackers' per annum and there is a full capacity output of 200 000.

(a)   State which of the above costs are fixed and which are variable.

fixed costs are time based

(b)   Calculate breakeven output per annum.

FC/Cont pu

(c)   Calculate the profit made at current and full capacity output.

profit = TR − TC

(d)   If Firezone Ltd had a target profit of £2 187 500 at the current level of output, what must the selling price be?

use above formula

Contributions and Breakeven

2 Study the breakeven chart below and answer the following questions.

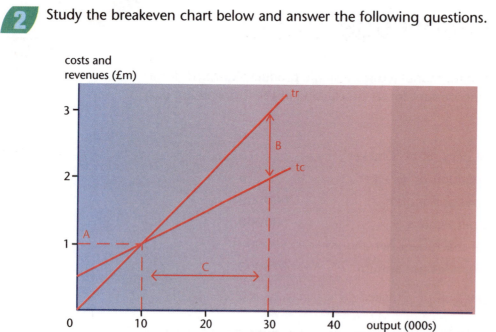

Hint

Note – current output is 30 000 units.

(a) What variable is measured at point A?

(b) What is measured by distance B?

(c) What quantity is measured by distance C?

(d) Demonstrate the new breakeven output if the selling price was increased to £125.

not BE output

measured in units

draw a new TR line

15 minutes

 **your knowledge**

 A balance sheet is a _____ of a firm's financial position at a specific point in time, whilst a profit and loss account is a measure of income over a _____ _____.

 A balance sheet has to balance the firm's _____ against its _____ and _____.

 A profit and loss account deducts _____ from _____.

 An expense that occurs because the cost of a fixed asset has to be spread over its useful life is known as _____.

 Fixed assets are generally shown in the balance sheet at their _____ _____ _____.

 Current assets minus current liabilities describe a firm's _____ _____.

 The section of the profit and loss account that calculates the gross profit is known as the _____ _____.

 A quantity that appears in both the trading account and the balance sheet is _____ _____.

 **Answers**

✔ **If you got them all right, skip to page 17**

30 minutes

Improve your knowledge

 The balance sheet is only applicable for the precise 'snapshot' moment in time at which it has been drawn up. Immediately after, transactions may occur which change several of the items in the balance sheet. By contrast, the profit and loss account is a historical document which remains a relevant measure of the surplus of revenue over cost for that time period.

 A balance sheet drawn up in horizontal format balances assets on the one side against capital and liabilities on the other.

 Profit is the difference between revenue and expenses.

 Depreciation is an application of the matching concept which states that costs and revenues must be matched together in the same accounting period. As a fixed asset lasts for several years, it would be breaching this concept if the whole cost was treated as an expense in the first year of use.

 Net book value is the remainder of the cost of the fixed asset after deducting all the year's depreciation charges to date. It would, of course, be pure fluke if this value corresponded to the current market value.

 Current assets minus current liabilities measures the working capital of a business, sometimes referred to as net current assets. This is an important measure for a business because it measures the ability to repay debts as they fall due.

 That part of the profit and loss account which records turnover and cost of sales is known as the trading account. It measures the gross profit, i.e. before overheads are deducted.

8 Certain items appear in both the profit and loss account and the balance sheet. One of these is the closing stock. This figure arises out of the end of year stocktake and is used to establish the value of the cost of sales for the year, but is also a current asset.

45 minutes

Use your knowledge

1 The following data refers to Tacky plc for the year ended 30 June 2000.

	£
Loan	150000
Stock	25000
Ordinary share capital	200000
Debtors	75000
Bank	50000
Cash	5000
Revaluation reserve	40000
Tax	15000
Retained profit	95000
Trade creditors	25000
Proposed dividends	25000
Land	175000
Buildings	100000
Vehicles	50000
Fixtures	70000

(a) Draw up a horizontal balance sheet as at 30 June 2000.

$A = L + C$

On 1 July 2000 the following transactions took place:

1 The dividends were paid by cheque.

2 £20000 of the loan was paid by cheque.

3 Shareholders purchased £50000 more share capital in the firm and paid by cheque.

4 The land was revalued at £200000.

5 New vehicles were bought for £10000 by cheque.

(b)   Draw up a balance sheet in vertical format as at 1 July 2000.

(c)   Calculate working capital and explain why this is an important quantity for a business.

(d)   Explain what is meant by a 'revaluation reserve'.

land and buildings

(e)   Why are most fixed assets depreciated each year in the accounts?

(f)   Why is land often not depreciated?

freehold

(g)   State three reasons why a balance sheet may not be an accurate valuation of the business at that date.

(h)   Why does retained profit appear on the balance sheet?

who does it belong to?

15 minutes

Test your knowledge

1 'Cash' refers to cash in notes and coins and also cash _____ _____.

2 Cash is the most _____ of all assets and thus has unique uses.

3 Good cash flow management can be seen as striking an acceptable balance between _____ and _____.

4 Cash flow involves time lags. A business wants the debtor's paying time lag to be _____ and the creditor's paying time lag to be _____.

5 If there are breaks in the cash flow cycle, the business may be unable to pay its _____ as they fall due and may thus face bankruptcy.

6 One way to improve cash flow is, rather than purchasing fixed assets, to _____ them instead.

7 Another is to establish proper credit control procedures, such as setting each customer a definite _____ _____.

8 Such procedures are not necessary if the business outsources its debt collection procedures, i.e. by appointing a _____ _____.

9 There is a very important difference between the net cash inflow for a business in a year and its reported _____ _____ for the same year.

Answers

1 at bank 2 liquid 3 liquidity, profitability 4 short, long
5 debts 6 lease 7 credit limit 8 debt factor 9 net profit

✔ **If you got them all right, skip to page 22**

30 minutes

 Improve your knowledge

 1 'Cash' is a wider term than just notes and coins – it also includes cash at bank. There is little to choose between these two with regard to liquidity.

 2 Cash is the most liquid of all assets and it is therefore uniquely placed to function as a universally acceptable means of exchange and, in particular, as the medium used to accept payments in settlement of debts.

 3 Liquidity and profitability are two conflicting aims of financial management. The former is vital to keep the business safe from insolvency, whilst the latter is necessary to attract capital providers to lend funds to the business.

 4 Some time lags are beneficial to a business whilst others are a hindrance. It is of benefit for the debtor's paying period to be short whilst the creditor's paying period is of benefit when long.

 5 Cash needs to be regularly and smoothly running through a business, often shown as a cash flow cycle. If there is an interruption to this flow, for example caused by a rash of bad debts, the survival of the business may be at risk as debts may not be paid as they fall due.

6 Major purchases of fixed assets, especially at the inchoate stage of a business, can act as a substantial drain on cash. Many businesses therefore prefer to lease them instead. Leasing illustrates the conflict between the objectives of liquidity and profitability, as it eases the strain on cash flow but probably works out more expensive in the long term.

 7 The adoption of appropriate credit control procedures helps to minimise the risk of suffering large scale bad debts. One part of this is to set each customer a credit limit based on perceived risk, size, references etc.

Cash Flow Management

 An increasing trend in modern business is for firms to employ the services of an external debt factor. The debt factor then shoulders much of the burden of the credit sales administration.

 A variety of reasons causes there to be an often substantial difference between net cash inflow for a period and reported net profit for the same period.

45 minutes

your knowledge

Hint

1 A company is in its first year of operation and has 150 000 £1 shares and a £25 000 bank loan at 15% interest.

In its first year it paid for the following items:

	£
Machinery	100 000
Raw materials	175 000
Wages	80 000
Overheads	30 000

Tax is 25% of net profit but, like the £15 000 dividends proposed, does not have to be paid until the second year. The company has paid £3750 interest on its loan.

Depreciation of machinery is a straight line, over ten years, with a zero scrap value.

During the year 1000 units of product were sold at £250 each, but 100 had not been paid for by year end.

Closing stock was £75 000.

(a) Calculate the cash balance at the end of the year.

(b) Calculate the profit carried forward to next year.

only cash movements

fair measure

2 Give three reasons why any firm's net cash inflow for a year may differ from its profit for the year.

Cash Flow Management

3 Give two reasons why a business would prepare a cash flow forecast.

Hint

not legally required

4 State two actions a firm could take to solve an immediate cash crisis.

5 If the company above was said to be 'overtrading', what would this mean?

6 Which of the possible company stakeholders is most concerned about liquidity as opposed to profitability? Explain your answer.

15 minutes

Test your knowledge

1 The budgeting process is part of the financial _____ procedure, whereby future expenditure is carefully forecasted for each department of the business.

2 The most sophisticated budgeting technique requires managers to justify all aspects of expenditure every year and is known as _____ budgeting.

3 It is important to set the budget targets at the correct level in order to maximise the _____ effect on the manager or employee.

4 Once budget targets have been determined, expenditure is _____ to see if there is any divergence from the amounts originally envisaged.

5 Any differences between budget and actual expenditure are recorded as _____ and the reasons for them must be investigated.

6 A segment or department of a business to which costs are traced and apportioned is known as a _____ centre.

7 A _____ centre is also able to trace its own revenues, so that it can function as a relatively autonomous business, with its own separate profit and loss account.

8 _____ are costs that are not uniquely associated with a particular product. They can be variable, though most are fixed in relation to the output level of the business.

Answers

✔ **If you got them all right, skip to page 27**

Budgeting and Cost/Profit Centres

30 minutes

Improve your knowledge

 1 Planning expenditure is crucial to the function of large organisations. If spending is unplanned it will prove to be difficult to control and contain. This will have an adverse impact on the profitability of the business.

 2 Zero budgeting seeks to successfully control expenditure and avoid the tendency of budgets to inflate gradually over a number of years. Unwarranted expenditure can be identified and eliminated through the justification process.

 3 The motivational or behavioural aspects of the budget process are said to be closely related to the magnitude of the targets set. Targets that are virtually impossible to reach, except in perfect conditions, are generally demotivating, whilst low targets can be achieved without significant effort. Challenging but feasible targets are generally believed to be the most motivating.

 4 Actual expenditure is carefully monitored to highlight departures from the budget figures. This is often performed on a monthly basis to keep a regular watchful eye on expenditure patterns. Seasonal variations are incorporated into the comparisons.

5 The monitoring process records departures of actual expenditure from the budget figures as variances. These can be of a favourable or adverse nature depending on the nature of the divergence. It is important that the causes of the variances are discovered quickly and remedial action taken.

6 Cost centres are created in order to strengthen the cost control process in an organisation. Instead of all costs being viewed as those of the whole organisation, they are traced or allocated to particular divisions of the business. In this way managers can be made responsible for the costs that arise in their cost centres.

Budgeting and Cost/Profit Centres

 Profit centres can be run as semi-autonomous divisions within a business. Managers here can be given responsibilities for costs and revenues within their centre and can therefore be given a profit target.

 Overheads can be of a fixed or variable nature. Most are fixed and typically include rent, business rates and insurance premiums. A smaller number are variable, such as energy sources like electricity. As fixed overheads are not linked to the activity of the business, they have to be apportioned to divisions using some rather arbitary allocation basis such as floor space or the number of employees.

45 minutes

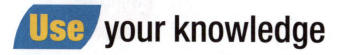 Use your knowledge

1 Provide definitions for:
(a) direct costs
(b) indirect costs.

2 Suggest two possible reasons for an adverse direct materials variance in a manufacturing company.

3 State three purposes of creating budgets.

4 Describe two possible sources of information for the creation of a sales budget.

5 Explain two difficulties involved in making correct budget predictions.

6 Evaluate the benefits of using zero budgeting in a business.

7 Discuss the advantages and disadvantages of apportioning fixed overheads to different profit centres within the business.

15 minutes

Test your knowledge

 1 A marketing strategy that consists of aiming one product at the whole market is known as _____ _____.

 2 A marketing strategy that consists of aiming different products at different segments of the market is known as _____ _____.

 3 _____ _____ is a third alternative which concentrates efforts on one small segment of the market.

 4 One approach to segmenting a market is to divide consumers into groups A, B, C1 etc., i.e. by their _____ _____.

 5 A more modern and sophisticated method that is increasingly popular is to segment a market by consumer _____, i.e. their habits and activities.

 6 Another approach based upon demographic patterns is to use _____ to segment a market.

 7 Different segments of a market require the use of contrasting styles of advertising, placed in quite different _____ _____.

 8 Failure to target promotions at the correct segmented audience results in a high degree of advertising _____, which is unproductive expenditure for a firm.

Answers

1 undifferentiated marketing   2 differentiated marketing
3 Niche marketing   4 social class   5 lifestyle   6 age
7 advertising media   8 wastage

✔ **If you got them all right, skip to page 30**

30 minutes

Improve your knowledge

 1 Undifferentiated marketing is sometimes described as mass marketing. The market is seen as so homogeneous that segmenting is either impossible or not worthwhile.

 2 Differentiated marketing is used when the market can easily be divided up into clearly defined segments based on one of a variety of characteristics.

 3 Niche marketing is where attention is concentrated on one very small part of a market, where there is perceived to be a gap. A firm entering a niche market can therefore enjoy a temporary absence of competition.

 4 This places consumers into a social class grouping based on occupation. For example, skilled manual workers are categorised as C2.

 5 Lifestyle is a richer concept than social class and encompasses, for example, attitudes, place of residence and choice of leisure activities.

 6 Age is an important divider as tastes and inclinations vary very considerably with it. Also, with constantly changing demographic patterns, it is important for firms to be aware of the impact this will have on the market for their products.

 7 Television and newspapers are examples of advertising media, but there are also crucially important differences *within* different elements of the same media. For example, between which programmes should an advertisement best be placed to reach a C1 audience?

 8 Wastage occurs when an advertisement fails to reach the designated target audience and instead reaches a different one.

45 minutes

Use your knowledge

1 Define the concept 'market segment'.

2 Give six characteristics which can be used to segment a market.

3 Explain the benefits to a firm of making use of market segmentation.

4 Give two advantages and two disadvantages of using a niche marketing strategy.

5 The Good Times Ltd holiday company is undergoing a fundamental review of its service portfolio and wishes to make full use of market segmentation in order to tailor its holidays to the various consumer requirements. Explain how the characteristics of:

(a)   age
(b)   lifestyle
(c)   social class

may be used to divide the holiday market into specifically identifiable market segments.

15 minutes

Test your knowledge

 1 There are no _____ in the development stage of the product life cycle, as this only includes the creation and design stage.

 2 The subsequent stages of the life cycle only occur if a decision is made to _____ the product.

 3 The _____ stage of the cycle occurs as sales start to peak and competitors threaten market share.

 4 At this stage, the life cycle may be prolonged by a variety of _____ _____.

 5 Product portfolio analysis divides products into four categories according to their current market _____ and market _____.

 6 Correct placement in the matrix makes it easier to devise appropriate expenditures on, for example, _____.

 7 A well established method of adding value to a product is to build up the weight of the _____.

 8 Product differentiation and market segmentation can serve to sharpen brand _____ and therefore make sales more resilient.

 **Answers**

✔ **If you got them all right, skip to page 34**

Product Life Cycle and Product Portfolio Analysis

30 minutes

Improve your knowledge

 1 The development stage precedes the introduction stage and therefore sales do not occur during this period. It is dominated by the investigation of creative ideas, designing according to declared design briefs and carrying out rigorous testing programmes.

 2 A launch of the product will only occur if the test marketing produces a favourable response. Launching a new product onto the market is inevitably risky, but well designed testing can significantly reduce that risk.

 3 Not all products follow the traditional bell-shaped pattern. Many, however, reach a maturity stage after a period of strong growth in which sales have increased rapidly. A mature product is approaching the peak of its sales which, by now, are only increasing very slowly.

 4 Extension strategies can be deployed to increase the length of a product's life cycle. They can be implemented as the product reaches maturity, when sales are no longer increasing so rapidly. Their aim is, at least temporarily, to deny the product the usual life cycle experience.

 5 The Boston matrix or box consists of four quadrants with differing combinations of market share and market growth. The 'star' product has a substantial market share in a rapidly growing market. The 'cash cow' is a mature product still enjoying good market share. The 'problem child' exists in a rapidly growing market but has yet to find popularity with consumers. The 'dog' has fallen out of favour with consumers in an already declining market.

 6 Correct positioning of products in the matrix is supposed to highlight appropriate marketing strategies and techniques, such as the correct amount of promotion expenditure. The model could be criticised, however, for assuming a rather mechanical marketing response to only two variables of market share and growth.

7 Brands are seen as crucial to the value-adding process. A brand is a name or symbol used to identify a particular product and distinguish it from those available from competitors. The price differential between between premium brands and supermarkets' own brands bears testimony to their value adding potential. Some of the top UK brands have been valued at hundreds of millions of pounds.

8 Brand loyalty reduces the price elasticity of demand for the product. This increases the power of the producer in relation to the consumer so that prices can be maintained or increased. Brand loyalty therefore constitutes a key weapon in the battle for added value.

Product Life Cycle and Product Portfolio Analysis

45 minutes

Use your knowledge

Hint

1 Sketch and label a typical product life cycle graph.

bell

2 Sketch and fully label the Boston matrix.

animals!

3 Distinguish between product differentiation and market segmentation.

4 Explain why increasing brand loyalty reduces the price elasticity of demand for a product.

PED formula

5 Define added value.

margin

6 What factors might limit the ability of a firm to add value to its products?

salt

7 Assess the usefulness of marketing models such as the product life cycle and the Boston matrix to real businesses.

15 minutes

Test your knowledge

1 When deciding on an appropriate pricing strategy, a business must decide what the main objective is to be. For example, is it to _____ _____ in the short term or is it to build up _____ _____ in the long term?

2 In very competitive markets, businesses may have very little influence over the price they can charge for their product. Such firms are therefore _____ _____.

3 For firms that are able to influence their prices, a variety of different pricing policies could be adopted:

(a) _____ _____ uses a low initial price to gain a foothold in the market and establish market share.

(b) The opposite approach of _____ _____ uses a high price to maximise profits whilst the product is at an early stage of its life cycle.

(c) A policy of _____ _____ identifies those segments of the market where demand is strongest and charges a premium price to those segments.

(d) An approach favoured by accountants is to use _____ _____ pricing, which identifies the full unit cost to make a product and then adds a mark-up for profit.

(e) _____ _____ uses a price below a product's cost of production in order to eliminate the competition from a market.

4 Whenever a business wishes to alter the price of a product it needs to consider the _____ _____ of _____. A value of less than one means a product with _____ _____. A value of more than one means a product with _____ _____.

✔ **If you got them all right, skip to page 37**

Pricing Strategies and Price Elasticity

30 minutes

 ## **Improve** your knowledge

1 If a firm wishes to maximise profits this implies a strategy that uses premium pricing, such as market skimming or price discrimination. If a build up of market share is sought, a policy such as penetration pricing, which undercuts the competitors, would be employed.

2 Firms are price takers where the market is so competitive that any excess charged over the market price leads to the complete loss of customers.

3 (a) Penetration pricing prices low to maximise sales.

(b) Market skimming prices high to maximise profit.

(c) Price discrimination splits customers into clearly defined groups in order to charge the maximum each group is able and willing to pay.

(d) Cost based pricing uses the absorption costing method of allocating overheads to products and then adding a suitable mark-up to obtain the final selling price. A drawback of this approach is that it is less market orientated than other methods.

(e) Predatory pricing identifies weaker rivals and charges a low price on a temporary basis with the aim of driving the rival out of the market, after which prices would be increased again.

4 Price elasticity of demand measures the responsiveness of the demand for a product to changes in its price. The formula uses percentage changes:

$$PED = \frac{\% \text{ change in quantity demanded}}{\% \text{ change in price}}$$

A value of less than one means that the percentage change in quantity demanded is less than the percentage change in price. Such a product is said to have inelastic demand.

A value greater than one means that the percentage change in quantity demanded outweighs the percentage change in price. This product would be said to have elastic demand.

45 minutes

Use your knowledge

1 Give two reasons why a product may have inelastic demand with respect to price.

cigarettes

2 A firm believes that its product has a PED of minus two. It is considering increasing the price from £20 to £25. The current level of sales is 500 units per week. State whether, and by how much, total revenue will change.

use PED formula

3 A firm makes three products, Tom, Jerry and Spike. It calculates its prices using the cost based pricing method.

	Tom	Jerry	Spike
	£	£	£
Direct costs (per unit)	100	50	200
Total sales in units	2000	5000	3000

Total overheads are £800 000 and these are to be split between the products on the basis of the level of sales of each product.

A mark-up on cost of 25% is to be added.

Calculate the selling price of each product.

allocate overheads in proportion to sales units

4 Why might it be unfair to split overheads on the basis of sales units?

15 minutes

Test your knowledge

1 The essence of Japanese lean production methods is for _____ _____ to be kept to the absolute minimum.

2 Instead of having a target of, for example, 3% failure rate in quality control, lean producers aim for _____ _____.

3 An approach to quality that encourages workers to see the recipient of their output as a 'customer', even when they are fellow employees, is known as _____ _____ _____.

4 _____-_____-_____ is the application of lean production philosophy to stock control systems.

5 The contrasting, traditional approach to stock control is to hold some _____ _____ as a safeguard against fluctuations in demand or supplier unreliability.

6 The level of stock at which a new request for a delivery takes place is known as the _____ _____.

7 If average usage of raw materials is 20 kg per week, buffer stock is 50 kg and the reorder level is 110 kg, calculate the lead time in weeks.

8 Absolute certainty of demand coupled with perfect reliability of suppliers may allow a manufacturer to hold a buffer stock of _____.

Answers

1 resource use   2 zero defects   3 total quality management
4 just-in-time   5 buffer stock   6 reorder level   7 three weeks
8 zero

✔ If you got them all right, skip to page 41

Lean Production and Stock Control

30 minutes

Improve your knowledge

1 Traditional mass production systems were seen as using an excessive quantity of inputs. Lean production seeks to keep resource use to the absolute minimum by reducing waste as much as possible.

2 Zero defects requires a quality target that has been realistically set, based upon an impeccable design and produced by very accurate and dependable production systems. It literally means perfect quality every time.

3 Total quality management depends on the creation of a 'culture of quality' which is supported by all management and employees. All functions within a firm are recast into relationships between an invented 'customer' and 'supplier'.

4 The just-in-time system minimises the various costs of holding stock by effectively abolishing the idea of a buffer or safety stock. This is consistent with the lean production philosophy of minimising waste. Space formerly used to store stock is now released for alternative purposes such as production.

5 Buffer stock is held as a hedge against sudden surges in customer demand or the failure of supplies to arrive at the expected time. More buffer stock is needed in uncertain situations, but this increases stock holding costs.

6 The reorder level is the level to which stock must fall in order to trigger a new requisition for supplies. In computerised stock control systems that use the EPOS principle, this reordering takes place automatically.

7   Buffer stock + lead time usage = reorder level
      50 kg   +   20 kg × 3   =   110 kg

8   As buffer stock is held as a hedge against a variety of uncertainties, a perfectly predictable environment would remove the need for it. Thus the safety stock could be zero and this is the ideal situation in which to use just-in-time.

Lean Production and Stock Control

Use your knowledge

1 State four key aspects of the lean production ethos.

2 State three costs of holding large quantities of stock.

3 Explain two advantages and two disadvantages of a firm changing to a computerised stock control (EPOS) system.

4 The diagram below shows a traditional stock control chart:

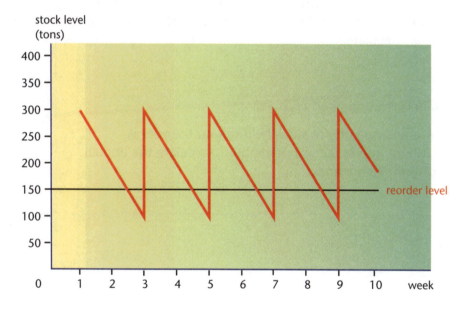

(a)   What is the average stock usage per week?

(b)   What is the level of buffer stock held?

(c)   How long is the lead time in weeks?

(d)   What is the size of each fortnightly delivery?

(e)   What would be the level of buffer stock if stock usage increased to 150 tons per week and the lead time became one week?

slope becomes steeper

5   A manufacturer uses 10000 kg each year of a raw material, AXMA, in the production of its products. The current price of AXMA is £5 per kilo. The lead time is two weeks, the order quantity is 2500 kg and buffer stock is 2000 kg. Assuming a 50 week year, calculate:

average usage during lead time + buffer stock = reorder level

(a)   the reorder level

(b)   the number of deliveries required each year

(c)   assuming the average quantity of stock held during the year is 3250 kg and a rate of interest of 6% per annum, calculate the annual opportunity cost of holding stock.

Test your knowledge

1. Human resource management sees _____ as a key resource in modern business organisations.

2. The aim of HRM is to manage and develop a firm's personnel in order to maximise the chances of achieving the firm's _____ _____.

3. An important emphasis of HRM is the need for organisations to encourage their employees continuously to invest in and develop their _____ _____.

4. Such investment in workers' capabilities is achieved through regular _____ programmes at frequent intervals to ensure workplace skills keep pace with technological change.

5. Training can often suffer from under-investment by firms because of the dangers of their staff, once better trained, being _____ by a rival company.

6. A high degree of _____ _____ is seen as a threat to the achievement of HRM goals because of its disruptive effects and the costs of regularly re-advertising posts.

7. HRM recognises the need to be aware of potentially far-reaching _____ _____ which mean that employers in the future may face a work-force with a significantly different age structure.

8. One way of regularly assessing the performance of staff is to engage in an annual _____ system.

Human Resource Management

Improve your knowledge

1 Human resource management is a spin-off from the various Japanese initiatives in managing people. Similar to the personnel function, it has a distinct emphasis on seeing people as one of many resources within a business, but having specific needs of its own. The aim is to manage human resources so that the firm can extract the maximum benefit from their deployment.

2 A firm's corporate objectives are the overall aims of the business and they are unlikely to be realised without the most productive deployment of a firm's human resources.

3 The productivity of any workforce is partly a function of the level of investment in its human capital. Not only should this increase a firm's productivity and effectiveness, it should also enhance the individual worker's earning power. Part of the remuneration of a highly skilled employee could be regarded as a return on the investment in that person's human capital.

4 Investment in human capital can be through either an education or training programme. On-the-job training enhances work-based skills and takes place at the usual workplace. Off-the-job training may be wider in scope and take place at a company national training centre.

5 Training carries a high degree of externalities in that, if provided for an employee by an employer, it can potentially benefit other rival firms. As most skills are portable with the employee, a competitor may, at some future stage, poach trained staff and thus benefit from the training provision as a free rider. This problem creates an inbuilt bias against an adequate national expenditure on training.

6 Firms that experience a high degree of labour turnover encounter a variety of problems. The regularity of staffing changes causes a major disruption to the organisation's business. Additionally, there are several wasteful expenses incurred, such as the costs of frequently retraining new staff and re-advertising vacant positions.

7 The 'demographic time bomb' describes the fact that the age structure of the workforce is likely to change significantly. Demographic changes mean that there will be fewer young people as a proportion of the workforce.

8 The annual appraisal interview is an opportunity for managers to review the effectiveness of each individual employee. Perhaps rather in conflict, annual appraisal interviews are also seen as an opportunity to assess performance, possibly linked to the size of a pay award, to identify training needs and to assist employees in reaching their full potential.

45 minutes

Use your knowledge

Hint

1 What is meant by the term 'empowerment'?

think power

2 What measures are taken to offset the inbuilt bias towards inadequate training?

3 State the formula used to measure the labour turnover in a firm.

turnover means leaving
Herzberg?

4 What are the possible causes of high labour turnover in a business?

5 What are the various drawbacks of high labour turnover for a company?

6 Describe the various ways a UK manufacturing company may alleviate the damaging effects of the 'demographic time bomb'.

7 What is the 'core and periphery' model of the labour market?

full-time/casual

8 Assess the advantages and disadvantages of a firm having a 'flexible' workforce.

Rewards and Remuneration

15 minutes

 Test your knowledge

1 The management theorist _____ _____ believed money to be the sole reason why employees turned up for work.

2 Pay systems founded upon such principles therefore attempt to find a way of linking an employee's pay to _____ of work undertaken.

3 A problem, however, with such 'piecework' type systems is that in many service sector occupations it is not easy to find a quantifiable measure of _____.

4 Modern remuneration systems based on these principles are therefore more sophisticated in their measurement of an employee's contribution to the attainment of the business's objectives. Such systems are described as _____ - _____ _____.

5 A key aspect of the contemporary pay scene is the government's introduction of a _____ _____ _____ of £3.60 per hour for adult employees.

6 Much of the controversy surrounding the introduction of this idea revolved around its possible impact on the UK level of _____.

7 By contrast there was also debate about whether there would be a positive impact on the level of employee _____.

8 The management theorist _____ _____ believed that whilst low pay was a serious demotivator, high pay did not necessarily have a positive effect.

 Answers

✔ **If you got them all right, skip to page 50**

30 minutes

Improve your knowledge

 1 **Frederick Taylor** created the scientific management school of thought with its associated work study methods. He believed the route to efficiency was a combination of piece-rate payment systems and tight management control.

2 Piece-rate payment systems seek to relate the financial rewards for an employee to the quantity of work.

3 Such systems are notoriously difficult to apply in the service sector due to the problem of identifying a suitable measure of output. In this sector, output is often of the 'invisible' kind and is qualitative rather than quantitative in nature.

4 **Performance-related pay** is a modern variant which seeks to reintroduce the financial calculus into an employee's motivation. It is usually awarded as a bonus or salary increase above the norm, following an appraisal interview.

5 The trades union movement had long campaigned for a national minimum wage to bring the UK into line with other advanced countries. However, they were disappointed at the relatively low level of the rate set.

6 Much of the opposition to the principle of a minimum wage is related to its alleged impact on the level of unemployment. In the diagram below:

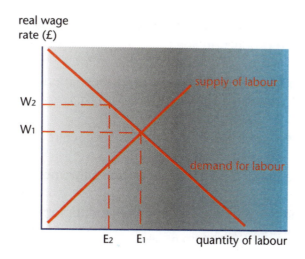

an increase in the wage rate from W1 to W2 reduces the employer's demand for workers from E1 to E2.

In this way, a minimum wage is said to 'price low-paid workers out of their jobs'.

However, the reality of the labour market is much more complex than this and the outcome depends on how other factors change in relation to the higher wage rate. For example, levels of training and productivity effects could enhance the demand for labour.

7 A higher hourly pay rate may create a greater feeling of employee motivation in the job. However, whether the employee gains financially depends on the degree to which they receive income-related state benefits such as housing benefit or family credit.

8 Frederick Herzberg believed that higher pay, whilst reducing the demotivating effects of low pay, failed to motivate an employee positively.

45 minutes

Use your knowledge

Hint

think quality

1 Give two disadvantages of using a piece-work payment system on a manufacturing production line.

2 Name two other theorists who did not believe money to be an effective motivator at work.

3 What were the five levels of the Maslow hierarchy?

4 Explain three non-financial ways to improve the motivation of employees.

5 Taylor favoured a fairly rigid 'division of labour'. Explain the meaning of this and outline its drawbacks.

6 What was the 'Hawthorne Effect' and what school of management did it create?

7 Why do many managers, particularly in small firms, continue to ignore 'Hawthorne'-type ideas in their own workplaces?

8 Assess the case for and against introducing a system of performance-related pay for nurses at an elderly persons' care home.

nursing is a profession

9 Consider the possible employer reactions to the introduction of the national minimum wage.

15 minutes

 your knowledge

 The manner in which the economy moves from boom to slump, in a predictable pattern over a number of years, is known as the _____ _____.

 A boom in the economy is characterised by rapid _____ _____ above the trend rate, which causes unemployment to fall.

 Changes in the overall economy are often caused by actions taken by governments or central banks. Monetary policy actions involve the manipulation of _____ _____.

 Recessions cause problems for businesses as customers become harder to find. However, there may be a consolation in that it becomes easier to _____ staff.

 In recessions, the businesses that suffer the greatest percentage fall in sales are those that produce products or services which have a high _____ _____ of _____.

 Businesses dislike inflationary conditions because if their costs are increasing, they may have to increase their selling prices to protect _____ _____.

 The rate of inflation is generally measured using the _____ _____ _____, which measures changes in the prices of an average consumer's shopping bill.

 Businesses cannot escape from broader economic conditions. They are the key element of the _____ environment in which they have to operate.

✔ **If you got them all right, skip to page 54**

30 minutes

Improve your knowledge

1 Alternatively described as the business cycle, the trade cycle shows economic fluctuations between boom and slump over a variable number of years. These fluctuations revolve around a general upward trend caused by technological change.

2 When economic growth is faster than the long-term trend of approximately $2\frac{1}{2}\%$, new jobs are created faster than old jobs are destroyed by technological change. Unemployment consequently decreases.

3 In the UK, monetary policy is conducted by the Monetary Policy Committee of the Bank of England. It meets once a month to set interest rates for the next month.

4 As personal disposable income declines in a recession, firms find it increasingly difficult to maintain sales. However, some of this economic pain may be alleviated by the fact that it is easier to recruit staff. The field of candidates is likely to be much wider and less remuneration is required to attract applicants.

5 Products with a high income elasticity of demand will suffer the greatest proportionate fall in demand as personal disposable income declines in a recession. Products with a high IED tend to be luxuries rather than necessities.

6 Rising costs exert pressure on profit margins unless the firm is in a strong enough position to pass on the higher costs to customers through higher prices. Whether the firm is able to do this depends upon the price elasticity of demand for their products. If this is high, an increase in selling price is likely to result in a substantial loss of customers.

Business and the Economy

 The Retail Price Index is the measure of inflation used for many purposes such as updating social security benefits and by trades unions when negotiating pay rises. An alternative measure exists, known as the 'underlying' inflation rate, which excludes mortgage interest from the index.

 All businesses have to operate within an external environment which is largely beyond their influence. The economy is a key element of this environment.

45 minutes

Use your knowledge

1 What is meant by the term 'cost push' inflation?

2 The Retail Price Index for a country, Tonga, is 334.7 in August 1998 and in September 1998 is 342.1. Calculate the percentage increase in prices over the two months.

3 Explain the term 'gross domestic product'.

4 Why might an increase in interest rates, implemented to reduce inflationary pressures, actually cause an increase in the RPI in the short term?

5 What is meant by 'structural unemployment'?

6 How might the policies designed to cure structural unemployment differ from those designed to correct cyclical unemployment?

7 Pilco Ltd manufactures leisure products and sells exclusively in the home market, but it does face considerable competition from imports. It has a high gearing ratio of 65% as a consequence of a substantial variable rate bank loan.

How might Pilco Ltd be affected by a sudden and significant increase in interest rates by the Monetary Policy Committee?

15 minutes

Test your knowledge

1 If a business decides to commence exporting a product after many years of selling it into its domestic market, there may be two additional complications to consider:

(a) a different marketing _____ (b) a different _____.

2 One way to alleviate some of the problems in 1 (a) is for a firm to employ the services of a foreign _____ who is familiar with local trading customs and practice.

3 A major problem of 1 (b) is the _____ it introduces in decisions that involve planning ahead.

4 An importer of raw materials who has purchased them on 1 August 2000, but does not have to pay for them until 31 October 2000, faces the risk of a _____ of sterling between the two dates.

5 One way the importer can remove the uncertainty is to enter into a _____ _____ _____ on 1 August 2000 which fixes the exchange rate which will be used for the conversion of 31 October 2000.

6 Exchange rates between different countries are determined, at any point in time, in the _____ _____ _____ by the forces of demand and supply.

7 If a country has a _____ exchange rate, its government is prepared to allow its external value to fluctuate every day, according to the relative demand for it.

8 Immediately after a devaluation of sterling, UK exporters can choose to reduce the price of their goods overseas or they can retain the previous price and enjoy higher _____ _____.

Answers

✔ **If you got them all right, skip to page 58**

30 minutes

Improve your knowledge

 1 Advertising in a foreign country can be difficult if the business is not familiar with the culture of that country. Advertising codes and standards vary widely between countries.

A different currency may be involved in the transaction, introducing an additional element of risk.

 2 The use of an agent can minimise the risk of selling into a foreign market. An agent is a third party commissioned to undertake the selling and distribution for a particular region.

 3 Conducting transactions in foreign currency introduces extra uncertainty into the exchange process. There is usually a time-lag in business transactions between entering into contracts and money changing hands. As currencies often fluctuate between the two dates, the profitability of a contract can be significantly altered.

 4 If there is a depreciation of sterling between 1 August 2000 and 31 October 2000, the importer will have to find more sterling to obtain any agreed amount of foreign currency. This would decrease the sterling profitability of the transaction.

 5 A forward exchange contract is one of a variety of hedging methods that can be used to remove exchange rate uncertainty. The foreign exchange is still not collected until 31 October 2000, but the exchange rate used is the appropriate forward rate quoted on 1 August 2000.

 6 The foreign exchange market is an international forum in which currencies are traded. Excess demand for a currency exerts upward pressure on its exchange rate whilst excess supply causes it to depreciate.

When a country has a floating exchange rate, the central bank abstains from intervention to influence its external value. The government thus takes a 'laissez-faire' attitude towards the level of the currency.

 An exporter, following a depreciation of its country's currency, could reduce its prices abroad to maximise penetration of that market. Alternatively, it could take a more short-term view and maintain the same price abroad but enjoy higher profit margins.

Use your knowledge

1. An exporter sells a product in the USA which costs £35 to manufacture in the UK (including profit). Currently the exchange rate is £1 to $1.60. If there is a 12.5% depreciation of sterling against the dollar, calculate the US price of the product in dollars, before and after the depreciation, assuming the depreciation was fully passed on to the US consumer.

multiply £s by 1.6

2. If, by contrast, the exporter maintained the original dollar price in the USA and the sterling profit margin was originally 20%, calculate the new sterling profit margin after the depreciation.

margin is a % of price

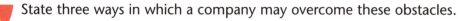

3. State three ways in which the marketing environment in a foreign country may differ from the domestic one.

4. State three ways in which a company may overcome these obstacles.

5. A manufacturer presently imports components from France. It believes very strongly that, over the next months, sterling is going to depreciate substantially against the franc. Suggest four ways the manufacturer can shield itself against such a movement.

hedging?

6. Explain the impact that a decision by the Monetary Policy Committee to increase interest rates may have on a company which exports half its output.

'hot money'

7. Assess the advantages and disadvantages for UK businesses of a future UK government decision to join the European single currency.

Exam Practice Questions

60 minutes

1 Smith and Jones is a firm of solicitors in the West Midlands. It has four branches which have quite wide variations in profitability. The revenues coming into each branch are broadly similar but the outgoings seem to be subject to considerable differences.

One of the senior partners, Mr Jones, has a background in accountancy. He feels that the firm needs to make much greater use of budgetary control and devolved financial management. He believes that the firm has been rather lax and indisciplined in this area in the past. In particular he is an enthusiast for zero-based budgeting which he argues would amount to a cultural change in the way budgets are established. The firm's current approach of using last year's budget plus an allowance for inflation, he contends, encourages wasteful expenditure.

The annual expenditure of one of the branches, Edgbaston, is shown below, analysed into five broad aggregates.

Year 2000	Budget (£)	Actual (£)
Rent	10 000	10 500
Staffing	80 000	90 000
Electricity and gas	2000	1600
Depreciation	5000	5000
Consumable items, e.g. paper	8000	8600

(a) Define the terms 'budgetary control' and 'devolved financial management'.
(4 marks)

(b) Calculate the variances for the year 2000, stating in each case whether they are favourable or adverse. (4 marks)

(c) Explain one possible cause and one possible solution for this cause for each of the variances above. (8 marks)

(d) Discuss the advantages and disadvantages of the application of 'zero-based budgeting' in the above type of business. (9 marks)

2 A small company, Adrax Ltd, has now been trading for a couple of years in the electronic components supply sector. This sector of the economy has become increasingly competitive over recent years and faces some quite ferocious international competition from lower cost producing countries.

Consequently, Adrax Ltd has had to try to carve out its own niche market within this sector and concentrate on high added value products. This strategy has been successful so far in terms of sales growth and market share, but has been costly in terms of capital equipment and human resources expenditure. This has put considerable strain on the company's cash flow situation.

For its third year of trading, Adrax Ltd has prepared the following sixth monthly cash flow forecast.

Cash inflow	Jan	Feb	Mar	Apr	May	June
Sales £	50000	52000	55000	60000	72000	58000
Cash outflow						
Staffing	20000	20000	25000	20000	30000	22000
Materials	15000	15000	15000	17500	20000	17500
Equipment	–	–	30000	–	40000	–
Miscellaneous	10000	?	12000	12000	15000	12000
Balance b/f	2000	7000	11000	(16000)	(5500)	(38500)
Balance c/f	7000	11000	(16000)	(5500)	(38500)	(32000)

(a) Define the term 'added value'. (2 marks)

(b) Calculate the miscellaneous expenses figure for February. (2 marks)

(c) Explain three differences between a cash flow forecast and a profit and loss account. (6 marks)

(d) Analyse the benefits Adrax Ltd may experience through preparing such a forecast. (7 marks)

(e) On the basis of the information above, account for and assess the financial position of Adrax Ltd. (8 marks)

Answers on page 86

Stakeholders and Objectives

(1) Profit-maximisation
(2) growth
(3) survival
(4) prestige
(5) director perks
(6) sales maximisation.

 The output where the vertical distance between total revenue and total cost is the greatest.

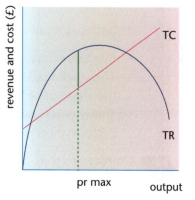

 Directors may be judged on their success at increasing sales rather than profits. Sales maximisation might therefore be better for their career prospects.

4 The output at which total revenue has peaked. Notice this is not the same as the profit maximising output.

 See diagram:

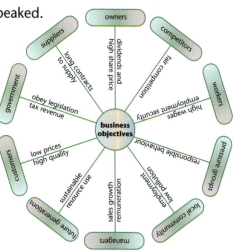

The issue only really arises in public limited companies where there is a divorce of ownership from control. Here the small class of directors may have interests that do not wholly coincide with the mass class of shareholders.

Arguments for:

- Shareholders are only interested in profits which lead to dividends and increases in the share price. Directors may have wider interests such as the prestige of the company name and maximising their own remuneration.
- Divorce of ownership from control makes this possible.
- Most shareholders have no contact with the company and thus can be easily hoodwinked.

Arguments against:

- Most directors also own shares and therefore will also be interested in profits.
- The stock market acts as a discipline forcing firms to maximise profits. Otherwise the share price falls, leaving the company vulnerable to takeover.
- Shareholders can remove directors at the AGM if they are not satisfied with their performance.

 Companies that narrowly follow the short term route to maximising shareholder value, it is argued, will be less successful because they will alienate the remaining stakeholders. For example, neglecting the labour interest will lead to a lower quality labour force. This could have very serious consequence given the increasing importance of human resources. The same could be said of other stakeholders.

Use your Knowledge Answers

Sources of Finance

 Some or all of the following could be used:
(1) credit reference agency checks; (2) customer's past conduct of bank account; (3) number of other creditors and amount owing; (4) security; (5) future prospects of type of business.

 Dividends and growth in the value of the share. Dividends are subject to income tax and capital growth is subject to capital gains tax.

 Advantages

(1) Helps cash flow. (2) Administration savings.

Disadvantages

(1) May reduce profit margin too much. (2) Loss of control over credit vetting process.

 (1) Fixed rate of dividend. (2) No vote at annual general meeting. (3) Priority return of capital on winding up of company. (4) No share in any surplus assets on the winding up of a company.

 Advantages

(1) No long term increase in return expected. (2) No dilution of existing voting rights at annual general meeting. (3) Corporation tax relief on debenture interest.

Disadvantages

(1) Increases gearing. (2) Danger of receivership if profits and cash flow collapse. (3) Vulnerable to increases in interest rates. (4) Interest cannot be waived unlike dividends.

 Dividends may not be paid if profits fall. Company may find it difficult to raise new finance.

 Capital expenditure is on long term fixed assets such as buildings or machinery. This would be tend to be financed by long term methods such as retained profits or loan or equity finance. Revenue expenditure is on items that will be consumed fairly quickly such as stocks or labour costs.

 (1) Retained profits. (2) Sale of fixed assets (perhaps to be leased back).

Contribution and Breakeven

(a) Variable: direct materials and direct labour.
Fixed: rent, rates, depreciation and insurance.

(b)
$$\text{BE output} = \frac{\text{fixed costs}}{\text{contribution per unit}} = 125\,000 \text{ units}$$

(c) *current output*

Profit	= total revenue	−	total costs
	= £60 × 150 000	−	[£4 375 000 + (£25 × 150 000)]
	= £9 000 000	−	£8 125 000
	= £875 000		

full capacity output

Profit	= total revenue	−	total costs
	= £60 × 200 000	−	[£4 375 000 + (£25 × 200 000)]
	= £12 000 000	−	£9 375 000
	= £2 625 000		

(d)

Profit	= total revenue	− total costs
£2 187 500	= P × 150 000	− £8 125 000
£10 312 500	= 150 000P	
£68.75	= P	

2 (a) Point A measures breakeven sales revenue. This is not the same as breakeven output and is measured in £s rather than units.

(b) Distance B measures the profit at output of 30 000 units.

(c) Distance C measures the margin of safety in units.

(d) An increase in the selling price will raise the gradient of the total revenue line. This new line will intersect with the total cost line at a lower breakeven output as shown on the next page.

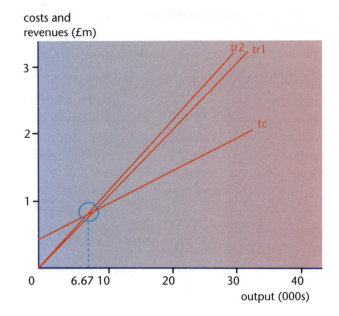

costs and
revenues (£m)

Answer = 6667 units

Balance Sheets and Profit and Loss Accounts

 (a)   Tacky plc Balance sheet as at 30 June 2000

	£		£
Fixed assets		*Capital and reserves*	
Land	175 000	Ordinary share capital	200 000
Buildings	100 000	Revaluation reserve	40 000
Fixtures	70 000	Retained profit	95 000
Vehicles	50 000		335 000
	395 000		
		Long term liabilities	
Current assets		Loan	150 000
Stock	25 000		
Debtors	75 000	*Current liabilities*	
Bank	50 000	Trade creditors	25 000
Cash	5 000	Tax	15 000
	155 000	Dividends	25 000
			65 000
	550 000		550 000

(b)   Tacky plc Balance sheet as at 1 July 2000

	£	£
Fixed assets		
Land		200 000
Buildings		100 000
Fixtures		70 000
Vehicles		60 000
		430 000
Current assets		
Stock	25 000	
Debtors	75 000	
Bank	45 000	
Cash	5 000	
	150 000	

Current liabilities		
Trade creditors	25 000	
Tax	15 000	
	(40 000)	
Net current assets		110 000
		540 000
Less long term *liabilities*		
Loan		(130 000)
		410 000
Capital and reserves		
Ordinary share capital		250 000
Revaluation reserve		65 000
Retained profit		95 000
		410 000

(c)   Working capital is £110 000. If this is insufficient it may mean that the firm is unable to pay its debts, which could lead to its enforced liquidation.

(d)   A reserve inserted into the shareholders' funds section to maintain balance after the upward revaluation of a fixed asset such as land, buildings or investments.

(e)   They generally have a finite life, and therefore an asset's cost must be spread over its useful economic life.

(f)   Freehold (i.e. outright ownership) land is available for an infinite number of years and there is thus no fixed life over which to spread the cost.

(g)   (1)   Goodwill is an intangible asset but is not generally shown on the balance sheet.

            (2)   Market depreciation rates may exceed those used to depreciate fixed assets in the accounts.

            (3)   Fixed assets such as land or buildings may not have been revalued for several years.

(h)   It increases the owners' capital and therefore must be added to it on the balance sheet.

Cash Flow Management

 (a)

	£
Cash inflow	
Share capital	150 000
Bank loan	25 000
Sales	225 000
	400 000
Cash outflow	
Interest	3 750
Machinery	100 000
Raw materials	175 000
Wages	80 000
Overheads	30 000
	(388 750)
Cash balance	11 250

(b)

	£	£
Turnover		250 000
Purchases	17 5000	
Closing stock	(75 000)	
Cost of sales		(100 000)
Gross profit		150 000
Less Expenses:		
Interest	3 750	
Wages	80 000	
Overheads	30 000	
Depreciation of mach.	10 000	
		(123 750)
Net profit		26 250
Less Appropriations:		
Tax	6 563	
Dividends	15 000	
		(21 563)
Profit cf		4 687

Use your Knowledge Answers

 (1)   Depreciation.

(2)   Credit sales and purchases.

(3)   Purchase or sale of fixed assets.

 (1)   To support an application for external finance.

(2)   To plan ahead for times of surplus cash.

 (1)   Negotiate new overdraft facilities.

(2)   Sale and leaseback of fixed assets.

 Expanding too rapidly without an adequate amount of working capital.

6 Probably creditors, as they are only interested in the repayment of the debt, plus an agreed amount of interest. They do not benefit from any surpluses.

Budgeting and Cost/Profit Centres

 (a) Direct costs are those that can be uniquely traced to a particular product.

(b) Indirect costs are overheads that are general to the business and cannot be so traced.

 Materials were acquired at a higher price than expected or more materials were wasted than expected.

 (1) To control costs.
(2) To motivate managers.
(3) To improve communication within the business.

 (1) Market research
(2) Past information within the business.

 Future demand patterns are uncertain and market research information is often unreliable.

 Advantages

Improves cost control. Eliminates inefficient activities and expenditure. Could lead to resources being released for other areas.

Disadvantages

It is very demanding of management time. Benefits may not always exceed costs of process.

 Advantages

A profit can be calculated for each division, which increases the accountability of managers. The profit calculations can be used to make decisions about whether to continue with the division.

Disadvantages

The method of overhead allocation may be unfair, which would demotivate managers. Fixed overheads apportioned from the whole business to divisions are often an irrelevant cost for decisions. This is because even if that particular division was closed the general business overheads would still have to be covered.

Targeting the Market

 1 A market segment is a small part of a market which has been divided up using one or more of the characteristics stated below.

 2
(1)   Age.

(2)   Sex.

(3)   Social class.

(4)   Geography.

(5)   Income.

(6)   Psychological attitudes.

 3 It allows a firm to penetrate a market in greater depth and obtain a larger degree of consumer identification with the product. Mass marketing promotion is rather bland, by comparison, because it is not possible to focus on particular types of consumers.

 4 Advantages

(1)   There is little, if any, specialist competition.

(2)   As only a small segment of the market is involved, a firm can really target its marketing efforts to a concentrated audience.

Disadvantages

(1)   It is risky because the firm has not diversified much and is therefore vulnerable to a collapse of its niche market.

(2)   Competition is likely to follow if the firm is successful in its operations.

5
(a)   E.g. SAGA-type holidays for the over 50s. Emphasis on guided tours, being looked after etc. Club 18–30 holidays for a younger market with emphasis on lively Mediterranean locations.

(b)   E.g. adventure type holidays for those with an outward bound lifestyle.

(c)   Five star hotel accommodation for social class A etc.

Product Life Cycles and Product Portfolio Analysis

 See diagram below.

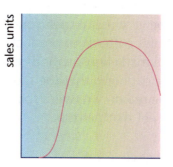

 See diagram below.

Market Share

		High	Low
Market Growth	High	Star	Problem Child
	Low	Cash Cow	Dog

 Product differentiation seeks to maximise the difference between a business's brand and that of its competitors. Market segmentation divides the market into different segments based on age, sex, etc.

 The formula for price elasticity of demand is

$$\frac{\% \text{ change in quantity demanded}}{\% \text{ change in price}}$$

Therefore the greater the brand loyalty, the smaller will be the % change in quantity demanded for any given price change.

5 Added value is an increase in the difference between the selling price and the cost of materials. Value is largely subjective so it is a means by which sellers are able to charge a higher price than previously.

Products that are very homogeneous, such as salt or sand, may present few opportunities as there is a limit to branding opportunities and advertising to niche markets.

 They can be very useful tools for marketing planning in that they can predict the likely sales patterns of products. Also they can provide guidance as to appropriate marketing methods according to how any product fits with this model. The danger is that the models can be applied too rigidly. They then become the reason why sales follow a particular pattern rather than an explanation of that pattern.

Pricing Strategies and Price Elasticity

1

(1)   There may be few substitutes for the product and therefore a price hike does not cause consumers to switch to an alternative.

(2)   The product may be strongly habit-forming and thus even substantial price increases do not deter many sales.

2

$$PED = \frac{\% \text{ change in quantity demanded}}{\% \text{ change in price}}$$

$$(-2) = \frac{Q}{25\%}$$

$$-50\% = Q$$

Therefore new quantity sold = 250 units per week.

New revenue = 250 × £25.00 = £6 250
Old revenue = 500 × £20.00 = £10 000

There is therefore a fall in revenue of £3 750.

This is to be expected with elastic demand |>2| as the percentage fall in demand will exceed the percentage increase in price.

3

	Tom £	Jerry £	Spike £
Direct costs (in total)	200 000	250 000	600 000
Overheads	160 000	400 000	240 000
	360 000	650 000	840 000
Total cost per unit (divide by sales)	180	130	280
Add mark-up of 25%	45	32.50	70
Selling price	225	162.50	350

Overheads, by their nature, are not generally related to sales as they are indirect costs. Overheads such as rent or business rates could be argued to be more a function of how much space a product occupies in the factory rather than of sales units.

If the firm uses cost-based pricing, then how overheads are allocated will affect the selling price and therefore the demand for a product.

Lean Production and Stock Control

1 (1)   Using the minimum of scarce resources.

(2)   Checking quality at all stages of production.

(3)   Empowering employees to check their own output.

(4)   Shorter product development cycles.

2 (1)   Storage.

(2)   Deterioration.

(3)   Interest lost on funds tied up in stock.

3 Advantages

(1)   The system is less vulnerable to human error.

(2)   Greater information is revealed, e.g. about consumer buying habits.

Disadvantages

(1)   Staff will need retraining in its use.

(2)   Expensive to purchase.

4 (a)   100 tons.

(b)   100 tons.

(c) $\frac{1}{2}$ week.

(d)   200 tons.

(e)   Zero.

(a) Reorder level = usage during lead time + buffer.

$$= \left(\frac{10\,000}{50} \times 2\right) + 2000$$

$$= 2400 \text{ kg}$$

(b) Number of deliveries $= \dfrac{\text{annual usage}}{\text{order size}}$

$$= \frac{10\,000}{2500}$$

$$= 4$$

(c) Opportunity cost = stock holding × cost per unit × interest rate
= 3250 × £5 × 6%
= £975

Human Resource Management

 Some extent of self-management, but within clearly defined guidelines. A means by which lower-level employees are allowed to exercise some discretion over the conduct of their work.

 Most countries use an extra-employer institution to oversee training, in recognition of the fact that an individual employer may not have sufficient incentive to provide an adequate level of training. That institution could be a government agency or it could be a voluntary body set up by the whole industry. A compulsory training levy is also sometimes used where all firms have to contribute to training and there is no opt-out option.

 Labour turnover = $\dfrac{\text{number of avoidable leavers per year}}{\text{average number of staff}} \times 100$

(1)   Low pay.
(2)   Poor career development structure.
(3)   Authoritarian management style etc.

(1)   Disruption to production.
(2)   Loss of experienced staff.
(3)   High retraining costs.
(4)   High recruitment costs etc.

6 A firm may have to change the typical target of its recruitment campaigns if there will be fewer young applicants. Various options are possible:

(1)   Aim more at women returners to the job market.
(2)   End age discrimination and remove maximum ages on job adverts.
(3)   Try recruitment abroad.

An approach to staffing where a 'core' of full-time, highly skilled, secure employees on attractive pay and conditions fulfil the essential roles within a firm. A 'periphery' of part-time casual workers on less attractive employment conditions are used to supplement the core at busier times.

 'Flexibility' can be seen as having a 'soft' and a 'hard' side. The soft side is not particularly controversial and uses multi-skilling and flexi-time to enjoy the benefits of an adaptable work-force. The hard side involves a deterioration in workers' employment conditions such as reduced sick pay and pension rights and short-term temporary contracts.

Advantages

(1)   Minimises costs.
(2)   Firm is able to respond to sudden changes in demand.

Disadvantages

(1)   'Hard' side flexibility may reduce morale.
(2)   Labour turnover may increase.

Rewards and Remuneration

(1) There is a danger that quality of output will suffer.

(2) Output may grow at times which suit employees' need for extra money, e.g. Christmas.

(1) Mayo,
(2) Maslow.

(1) Self-actualisation
(2) Esteem
(3) Social
(4) Safety
(5) Biological.

(1) Empowerment.
(2) Consultation.
(3) Flatter organisational structures.

A division of labour is a rigid demarcation of tasks where each employee contributes only a small repetitive part to the finished product. A high degree of specialisation is achieved which can increase productivity.

The drawbacks are the impact on motivation as the endless repetition of small tasks can be monotonous. Also many theorists have emphasised the 'principle of closure' whereby each worker sees a clear end product.

The 'Hawthorne Effect' spawned the 'human relations' school of management. Experiments conducted in the USA by Mayo found an improvement in productivity as a result of management interest in employees' work.

7

(1)	Ignorance of the research.
(2)	Scepticism about its validity.
(3)	Costs and disruptive effects of its implementation.

8

Advantages

(1)	A direct link between output and remuneration.
(2)	Hard working employees will be rewarded.

Disadvantages

(1)	It may be difficult to establish a sufficiently comprehensive measurement of 'performance' in this type of service industry.
(2)	May lead to certain activities being emphasised more than others.
(3)	Erodes the ethos of professionalism.

9

(1)	Reduce staffing levels and use machinery instead.
(2)	Reduce staffing levels and make the remaining staff work harder.
(3)	Maintain staffing levels and accept lower profits.
(4)	Maintain staffing levels and increase prices.
(5)	Invest in training to increase the productivity of now more expensive staff.

Business and the Economy

1 'Cost push' inflation is an upward pressure on prices caused by an increase in the cost of some input into production. Common examples are wages and raw materials.

2 % Increase $= \dfrac{342.1 - 334.7}{334.7} \times 100$

$\qquad = 2.2\%$

3 'Gross domestic product' is a measure of the output of the economy as a whole.

4 Mortgage interest rates are a constituent element of the RPI and therefore will cause it to rise. This is the reason many observers (including the MPC) prefer to follow movements of 'underlying inflation' which excludes mortgage interest.

5 Structural unemployment is brought about by the long-term decline of a particular industry such as Cornish tin mines or shipbuilding.

6 The usual remedy for cyclical unemployment is some technique of demand management. However, for structural unemployment the policy needs to be more narrowly focused on an industry and/or region. Examples are retraining schemes or regional development policy.

7 Pilco Ltd will face an increase in interest costs as it is highly geared. It will also face intensified competition from imports as the higher interest rates in the UK are likely to cause a stronger pound. In addition, it may suffer from a collapse in consumer demand as leisure products have high income elasticity of demand. Disposable incomes fall as there are higher costs of servicing mortgages.

The International Dimension

1 Pre-devaluation price was £35 × 1.6 = $56

Post-devaluation price is £35 × 1.4 = $49.

2 US price stays at $56.

This converts into £40 sterling ($56 / 1.4).

Cost of production is £28 (£35 × 0.8)

New profit is therefore £12.

$$\text{Profit margin} = \frac{\text{profit}}{\text{selling price}} \times 100$$

$$= \frac{£12}{£40} \times 100$$

$$= 30\%$$

3 (1) Cultural differences.

(2) Language differences.

(3) Political differences.

4 (1) Appoint an agent.

(2) Set up foreign franchises.

(3) Set up foreign production facilities.

5 (1) Purchase the francs now.

(2) Enter into a forward exchange contract now.

(3) Purchase the raw materials now.

(4) Find an alternative supplier in a different country.

Higher interest rates in the UK will attract an inflow of 'hot money' into the UK which will increase the value of sterling. This gives the company an uncomfortable choice of either increasing their export prices or absorbing the change through lower profit margins.

 ### Advantages

(1)   Elimination of conversion costs for trade with other Euro participating countries.

(2)   Removal of uncertainty about exchange rates with Euro participating countries.

(3)   Greater transparency of transactions enabling an easier search for the cheapest supplier.

Disadvantages

(1)   Economic policy determined by European central bank which will not be made with uniquely UK interests in mind.

(2)   Competition from other Euro countries is likely to be more severe in the UK home market.

1 (a) Budgetary control: comparing budget and actual figures. Devolved financial management: delegating budgets to lower management.

(b)
Rent	£500 (adverse)
Staffing	£10 000 (adverse)
Electricity and gas	£400 (favourable)
Depreciation	–
Consumables	£600 (adverse)

(c) Rent: rent has been increased; find cheaper premises. Staffing: extra staff employed; reorganise internal management. Electricity and gas: warmer weather than expected; no action needed. Consumables: higher than expected wastage; communicate with staff.

(d) Challenges all expenditure so helps to eliminate waste. Greater involvement of staff in budget process. More realistic and accurate budgets. However, a very time-consuming process.

2 (a) An increase in the margin between selling price and cost.

(b) £13 000.

(c) (1) Cash flow forecasts are not a legal requirement.
(2) They predict the future rather than describe the past.
(3) They measure liquidity rather than profitability.

(d) May help internal management of business. Acts as guideline for future. Highlights periods of cash surplus and deficit. Often required by external finance providers.

(e) Seems to be some seasonal pattern. Liquidity position seems to be deteriorating. Overdraft facilities needed from March. Get authorisation in advance. Equipment purchases are not spread at all.

Notes

Notes